Succeed at Stock Investing Even if You Don't Know Where to Start!

by Dr. Scott Brown

WORRY FREE WEALTH

Succeed at Stock Investing Even if You Don't Know Where to Start!

Explore the best mid and high yield diversified and focused strategies yielding 9 to 20% expected returns.

Disclaimer: The data contained herein is believed to be reliable but cannot be guaranteed as to reliability, accuracy, or completeness; and, as such are subject to change without notice. We will not be responsible for anything, which may result from reliance on this data or the opinions expressed herein.

Disclosure of risk: The risk of loss in trading stocks, futures, forex, and options can be substantial; therefore, only genuine risk funds should be used. Stocks, futures, forex, and options may not be suitable investments for all individuals, and individuals should carefully consider their financial condition in deciding whether to trade. Options traders should be aware that the exercise of a long option would result in a futures or forex position.

Hypothetical performance results have many inherent limitations, some of which are described below. No representation is being made that any account will, or is likely to, achieve profits or losses like those shown. In fact, there are frequently sharp differences between hypothetical performance results and the actual results subsequently achieved by any trading program.

One of the limitations of hypothetical performance results is that they are generally prepared with the benefit of hindsight. In addition, hypothetical trading does not involve financial risk, and no hypothetical trading record can completely account for the impact of financial risk in actual trading. For example, the ability to withstand losses or to adhere to a trading program, despite trading losses, are material points which can also adversely affect actual trading results. There are numerous other factors related to the markets. In general, or to the implementation of any specific trading program which cannot be fully accounted for in the preparation of hypothetical performance results and all of which can adversely affect actual trading results.

As costs vary among traders, including commission and fees, hypothetical trading examples usually do not always take commissions and fees into consideration. Please make sure you consider your individual cost of doing business in the form of commissions and fees.

TABLE OF CONTENTS

GOALS

At the end of my training, you will be able to...

1. Mind map the essential aspects of stock investing.
2. Implement the best diversified strategies.
3. Explore concentrated strategies.

Who should (or should not) take this course?

All saving heads of households should take this course.

What will students need to know or do before starting this course?

Basic reading and arithmetic.

How an Unskilled Minimum Wage 18-Year-Old Becomes a Millionaire+ by 60

I recently interviewed one of the three most **famous** value investors in the world. The first **two** are Warren Buffett and Charlie Munger.

Mohnish Pabrai draws **wisdom** from both. He describes a **librarian** who died with an estate of $4 million. The librarian **donated** it to the University of New Hampshire (UNH) in 2015.

http://www.cnbc.com/2016/09/20/librarian-leaves-4-million-to-alma-mater-critics-question-how-school-spends-money.html

Mohnish explains that any normal eighteen-year-old with very few skills who can only get a minimum wage job can make it.

The young McDonald's worker earns minimum wage of $15,000 for 2,000 hours of work per year. He can save ten percent because he is **living** at home and contributing 90% to the household budget.

The young man sets aside ten percent of $15,000 before **taxes** each year. The 18-year-old **saves** $1,500 each year into a Roth (after taxes) or employer sponsored IRA (before taxes).

This is a **conservative** example. The young man (for ease of example) does not get a boost from employer matching if he saves in an employer sponsored 401(k). This would allow him to save much **more**.

He earns 9% on a simple investment choice. His income rises modestly with **inflation**. For instance, if inflation is 2% this year he will save $1,530 in the **next**.

When he **retires** 50 years from now at the age of 68 he will have saved $75,000 over the years from his salary.

At 9%, the account **doubles** every 8 years as per the rule of 72. The approximate time to double an account is the number 72 divided by the rate of return on the investment.

How Much Does $75,000 of Drip Savings Grow at 9% in 50 Years? Answer: $1,332,662

Bankrate.com has a **calculator** that shows that this scenario will produce a retirement account for the unskilled, minimum wage 18-year-old of $1,332,662:

http://www.bankrate.com/calculators/retirement/traditional-ira-plan-calculator.aspx

Is this reasonable?

The most **respected** textbook on investments is "**Essentials of Investments**" by professors Bodie, Kane and Marcus. The chapter on portfolio theory **reports** that a portfolio of small U.S. stocks returned 11.80%, large U.S. stocks returned 9.62%, and world stocks 9.21%.

These are the geometric mean **returns** that investors enjoyed from 1920 to 2010 in the stock market.

A simple exchange traded fund such as the **Diamond – SPDR Dow Jones Industrial Average (DIA)** would have allowed this unskilled 18-year-old to capture a large stock return of 9.62% over that period.

The financial **success** of this 18-year-old comes from the power of compounding over a long time. The Pabrai fund has generated average **returns** of about 15%.

This higher return would generate a $12,450,561 **portfolio** for the eighteen-year-old. A difference of just over 5% produces a fortune nearly **ten** times greater!

Welcome to Succeed in Stocks Even if you Don't Know Where to Start! I want to be the first to congratulate you on showing that you are a cut above. The Federal Reserve discovered that only 43.8% of households are invested in the stock market.

What you are about to learn has allowed us to build a massive retirement stock portfolio. Just follow the simple steps you will learn. Enroll now in the free Udemy companion training to this kindle for videos and test banks, https://www.udemy.com/succeed-in-stocks-even-if-you-dont-know-where-to-start/

I am here to answer your questions. -Doc Brown

P.S. I put my heart and soul into this training. I am not a Hollywood documentary producer. If there is something you don't like about this course, please send me a personal message at support@worryfreewealth.com rather than giving the course a bad rating. Give me a chance to fix the problem first. Sincere thanks on this.

CURRICULUM:

Dr. Scott Brown Welcomes you to this Training

How to Get the Most Out of this Training

I am Dr. Scott Brown. I hold a coveted Ph.D. in finance from a good school, **The University of South Carolina**. I am also a leading researcher and tenured professor of Finance at the AACSB Accredited Graduate School of Business of the University of Puerto Rico.

I am teaching this course to give you a firm base for managing your family stock portfolio. I have discovered that few investors grasp the **big picture** required to successfully handle difficult questions with your hard-earned savings.

The typical student of this course has a **successful career** and is saving money to invest in a retirement. He or she doesn't have a background in finance or economics. That said this course is excellent for anybody interested in stock investing.

This subject is important because **households** today are forced to manage their retirements independently of the firm for which they work. You are helped to open a 401(k) or another retirement plan. But nobody is there to assist you in selecting the assets you will need to retire wealthy.

In this **course**, you will learn,

Section 1: Putting the Stock Market to Work for You!

Section 2: Discovering the Proven Best Strategies to Beat the Market!

There are **three student benefits** that are important to keep in mind.

1. The first benefit is that you will tap the returns of stocks, stock mutual funds and ETFs that have been proven to offer the most potential for growth over the long term as compared to bonds.
2. The second benefit is that if you invest with patience you can ride out market crashes.
3. The third benefit is that you can alternate between stocks, cash, and bonds.

At the end of this course, students will be able to implement the best diversified strategies yielding 9 to 10% expected returns. Explore concentrated strategies with 18 to 20% average anticipated yields to decide if these are right for you.

SECTION 2:

Putting the Stock Market to Work for You!

The stock market offers main street the highest expected returns on Wall Street.

LECTURE 1:
Life Changing Returns

Life Changing Returns

In August of 2004, Google went public, auctioning its shares in an unusual IPO format. The shares sold for $85 share, closing at over $100 on day 1. At the beginning of 2017 Alphabet Inc. (GOOG) was trading at $801 per share across the NasdaqGS per Yahoo.

This represents a gain to an investor of $716 per share.

Thus $85,000 invested into 1,000 shares in 2004 represents $716,000 today in liquid net worth of Alphabet Inc. (GOOG) stock. This course is designed to show you how to put yourself in the path of such possibilities.

In this training, you'll discover...

- Stock Market Indexes and put them to work for you.
- How the Stock Market is Regulated
- How to Theoretically Estimate the Fair Price of Common Stock
- How the Market Prices Common Stock in Reality
- The Source of Errors in Valuation that Lead to Severe Losses
- How to Invest in Domestic or Foreign Stocks

What is a Share of Stock?

A share of stock is ownership in a firm. Shares confer voting rights for directors and some additional decisions managers should not be trusted to make. These include amendments to the corporate charter and the issuance of new shares.

Most investors purchase common stock in companies trading across major exchanges.

These offer you the best opportunities by far because people know a lot about these companies. There are only two ways to make money in common stocks.

Profit #1: Share prices can rise over time. These profits are called capital gains.

Profit #2: The company can pay a part of the earnings from company assets to the owners. These are called dividends.

There are two types of stock. The first is common. The second is preferred.

Preferred stock pays a fixed dividend. Preferred stock holders do not vote.

Claims on firm assets by stock investors are subordinate to those of bond owners. For this reason alone, stock is riskier than bonds.

Stockholder residual claims are the rights to firm assets when bust. This means that stock investors are last in line after creditors to clean the meat off a bankrupt firm.

Bonds mature and are paid off. A share of stock exists for as long as the firm remains solvent.

It is very unlikely that an investor can get rich starting with small amounts of savings even though bonds are less risky. Common stock on the other hand is the best vehicle for growing rich from meager savings.

Notice that this stock certificate has no maturity, par (face) value, or interest rate. That is because this is a certificate for fifteen shares of common stock. The CUSIP number is a unique firm identifier. A CUSIP is assigned by the, *"Committee on Uniform Securities Identification Procedures. The CUSIP number identifies a financial instrument, including: stocks of all registered U.S. and Canadian companies, commercial paper, and U.S. government and municipal bonds."*

Common stock differs along two dimensions: voting rights, and dividends.

If the certificate listed a maturity, par, or interest rate you would immediately assume it to be preferred stock. That is because preferred stock pays a constant dividend.

Preferred stock does not confer voting rights.

This makes preferred stock as much like a bond as a share of equity. This softens the price volatility of preferred stock.

In bankruptcy, preferred stock holders recoup their investment before common stock holders but after bond holders.

Just a small fraction (5%) of capital is raised through preferred stock because the dividend payments are not tax deductible — as are bond interest payments. It costs the company more money to issue preferred stock than it does to sell bonds.

Billions of shares transact daily across the stock exchanges in the United States. This generates an orderly flow of capital, equity, and information to you as investor.

Order is a key feature of well-developed and efficient stock markets that attracts investors to trade. Electronic trading is muscling out both organized exchanges and traditional over-the-counter dealer networks.

The New York Stock Exchange (NYSE) is the best known, with daily volume of around 4 billion shares. This volume can peak at 7 billion shares traded in a single daily session. The NYSE started with twenty-four brokers in 1792 from a Manhattan coffee house called the Tontine on the north-west corner of Wall and Water.

Nicknamed the big board, it is still the largest and the most liquid in the world. It is a specific location where buyer and seller meet on a regular basis to trade securities in open-outcry.

Only the largest stocks can trade across the NYSE. A firm must have at least $10 million in earnings per year and $100 million in market value (cap).

The average today is more than $19.6 billion in market value.

Open-outcry is fading away. Computer systems (ECNs) have replaced the floor auction.

The NYSE today is a hybrid exchange that operates electronically through the Archipelago off the floor. More than 8,000 firms list across the Archipelago merged NYSE Euronext electronic communication network (ECN).

The NYSE hit a major milestone on October 28, 1998 when volume topped 1 billion shares. This was amazing two decades ago but the stock market is still growing. Consider this.

The average daily volume in 2013 was more than 4 billion shares per day.

Regional exchanges such as Philadelphia are easier to list across and welcome small firms. Some firms list across multiple exchanges. Some managers prefer the exposure of listing across the big board.

There is no evidence that listing a company across a prominent exchange helps the share price. Microsoft (MS) had a market cap of more than $250 billion at the beginning of the century but has never listed across a prominent exchange.

The two other major world exchanges besides the NYSE include,

- London Stock Exchange (LSE) in England.
- Tokyo Stock Exchange (Nikkei) in Japan
- Minor international exchanges include,
- Frankfurt Stock Exchange (DAX) in Germany
- Toronto Stock Exchange (TSE) in Canada
- Sydney Stock Exchange (ASX) in Australia.

There are many others but you should focus your attention on those in the United States first. These are the strongest leaders.

Over-the-counter markets

A company can list its stock on a network of dealers. The best example is the **National Association of Security Dealers Automated Quotation System (NASDAQ)**.

This was started in 1971 and allows dealers to make a market for a small stock. The movie Wolf of Wall Street described exactly how this is done.

Today, 3,100 different stocks are listed across the NASDAQ.

This is an important market for thinly-traded securities—securities that don't trade very often. Without a dealer, ready to make a market in small cap stocks these would be difficult to trade.

History was made when Facebook (FB) listed across the NASDAQ in 2012. The volume was so high that the quotation system collapsed under the strain.

Facebook (FB) dropped into the forties where it became a great investment.

Investing in Stocks: Organized vs. OTC

Organized exchanges (e.g., NYSE) use auction markets with floor specialists who quote through open outcry. A quarter of all trades are filled directly by a specialist.

Nine tenths of the trades cross buyer with seller.

Ten percent are the specialist buying and selling for his or her own account. The specialist system has been widely criticized as giving a few dealers an unfair advantage.

Two thirds of trades are filled through SuperDOT. The Super Designated Order Turnaround System (SuperDot) is an electronic order routing system for traders under 100,000 shares with priority on order sizes below 2,100 shares.

Over-the-counter markets (e.g., NASDAQ) use market makers who post bid and ask prices on stocks that are thinly traded. This is important to the economy.

Each stock has a reasonably fair price due to market makers. This argument does not extend to specialists.

Multiple market makers offer bid and ask prices on a specific stock.

Investing in Stocks: ECNs

ECNs (electronic communication networks) facilitate transactions between brokers and traders without a middleman; specialist or market maker. Instinet and Island compete with NYSE Euronext. These offer:

Transparency: Some allow traders to see the full limit order book where everyone can see unfilled orders. Not all ECNs do so. Some are less transparent than others.

- **Cost reduction**: Smaller spreads come without specialists or middlemen.
- **Faster execution**: ECNs offer the fastest fill times per trade.
- **After-hours trading**: An ECN allows you to trade stocks after hours on information releases.

ECN Drawbacks

ECNs have problems. They don't work for thinly-traded stocks where long periods pass without a transaction. There is also a lot of competition for volume among ECNs.

This makes it unclear which will thrive.

Investing in Stocks: ETFs

Exchange Traded Funds were created in 1990 to offer stock investors access to exotic investments and slash transaction costs. Within a decade from the introduction of the first over a 1,000 existed.

You will focus on a small group of the most liquid. These are less than 50.

Each represents a basket of assets ranging from physical commodities to financial securities. ETFs are traded across major exchanges.

The ETF indexes to a specific portfolio such as the S&P 500 or COMEX Gold. This minimizes management fees. The first, foremost, and largest indexed mutual fund to date is the

Vanguard 500 Fund (VFINX) offering expected returns between 9 and 10%.

These returns can easily be replicated using the ETF SPDR (SPY). ETFs have lower management fees than indexed mutual funds.

The extended market indexed mutual fund has an expense ratio (cost) of 0.25. The ETF has a cost of 0.08.

Investing in VFINX is the easiest way an unskilled worker can become a millionaire in the opening example of this course. There are

- Spiders
- Vipers
- Diamonds
- Qubes

ETFs cover virtually every sector and asset in the market today.

LECTURE 2:

Equity Pricing Theories

Pricing Common Stock

Common stock valuation is easy to calculate. Identify cash flows and discount them to the present.

Let's review 4 different methods for valuing stock. Each has advantages and drawbacks.

The One-Period Valuation Model

This simple model incorporates the dividend and price investors expect over the following year.

$$\text{Price} = \frac{Div_1}{(1 + k_e)} + \frac{P}{(1 + k_e)}$$

The One-Period Valuation Model Example

Here is an example using the expected dividend and price figures over the next year. What is the theoretical price for a stock with an expected dividend and price next year of \$0.16 and \$60? Using a 12% discount rate the answer is \$53.71.

$$\text{Price} = \frac{0.16}{(1 + 0.12)} + \frac{60}{(1 + 0.12)} = 53.71$$

The Generalized Dividend Model

This model uses all dividend payments and no price. It assumes that the value of the stock is comprised of a series of dividends.

Many stocks do not pay dividends now. Most of these companies start issuing dividends once rapid growth of the firm life-cycle has been passed. Notice that summation is infinite,

$$\text{Price} = \sum_{t=1}^{\infty} \frac{Div_t}{(1 + k_e)^t}$$

Gordon Growth Model

The infinite sum may not be tractable. The Gordon growth model is a simplification that makes it easy to estimate the generalized dividend model.

$$Div_{(t+1)} = Div_t \times (1 + g)$$

$$\text{Price} = \sum_{t=1}^{\infty} \frac{Div_t}{(1 + k_e)^t} = \frac{D_1}{(k_e - g)}$$

The Gordon Growth Model

The model assumes that dividends grow forever. Dividends are indeed "sticky" in that they tend to go up. The growth rate of dividends, g, is assumed to be less than the required return on equity, k_e. Otherwise the dividend growth rate for the firm would become unrealistically large.

The Price Earnings Valuation Method

Many firms do not pay dividends. An alternative to dividend growth models is the price earnings ratio (PE), This is a widely-watched ratio that explains how much the market is willing to pay for $1.00 of firm earnings. It is simple to compute. Multiplying the average industry P/E time the expected earnings per share. This calculates the value estimate of the stock share price.

$$\text{Price} = \frac{P}{E} \times E$$

Computing the Price of Common Stock

The industry PE ratio is 16 for a firm. What is the current price to earnings valuation method stock price for a firm with earnings of $1.13 / share?

Answer: The value (price) of the firm is the P/E ratio times earnings.

Price = 16 X $1.13 = $18.08

Investors interpret a higher-than-average PE as anticipation of higher future earnings. A high PE ratio can also be from a perception that firm earnings are very secure.

SECTION 3:

Discovering the Proven Best Strategies to Beat the Market!

These simple portfolios offer the highest expected returns.

PART 1:
How Mr. Market Sets Security Prices

How Mr. Market Sets Security Prices

Prices are set as the price the buyer is willing to pay for an asset in a competitive market. Superior information can play an important role in setting asset prices. Undervalued assets are bid up. Overvalued assets are bid down.

How Mr. Market Sets Security Prices

Imagine you go to a used car auction. You find a Honda Accord you drive to inspect before the auction.

It rattles a bit but you decide it is worth $5,000.

A mechanic is at the auction and drives the car as well. He realizes that the rattling is just brake pads that are cheap to fix.

He decides it is worth $7,000.

You are the only two bidders. You open with a bid of $5,000.

The mechanic bids $5,100.

You stop bidding because this is over your perceived value. The car is sold for $5,100 to the person willing to pay the highest price for the asset.

Imagine a stock that will pay $2 next year and grow for 3% forever. You require a 15% rate of return to compensate yourself for risk that the dividend and growth rate could drop or disappear.

Jennifer is more confident that both the dividend and growth rate is sustainable. As such, she only needs a 12% return to compensate herself for risk of dividend and growth reduction.

Bud works in the industry as a highly competent engineer and knows what the future of the firm is. He sees virtually no risk in his investment and requires just 7% to compensate for his risk.

Notice the wide range in values each investor will assign to the stock price. You will be willing to pay no more than $16.66 per share. Jennifer will pay up to $22.22. And Bud will pay as much as $50 per share.

The net effect is that the price of the stock will get bid up to $50 per share.

Investor	Discount	Price
You	15%	$ 16.66
Jennifer	12%	$ 22.22
Bud	7%	$ 50.00

Valuation Errors

Lots of problems mess up the Gordon model.

1. Estimating Growth
2. Estimating Risk
3. Forecasting Dividends

Dividend Growth Rate Errors

Stock Prices for a Stock with D_0 = $2.00, k_e = 15%, and various growth rates. Estimation error can be huge!

Growth (%)	Price (%)
1	14.43
3	17.17
5	21.00
10	44.00
11	55.50
12	74.67
13	113.00
14	228.00

Stock Prices for a Stock with D_0 = \$2.00, k_e = 5%, and various growth rates. Estimation error dramatically impacts required return.

Required (%)	Price ($)
10	42.00
11	35.00
12	30.00
13	26.25
14	23.33
15	21.00

The Scientific Art of Stock valuation

Considering different growth rates and required rates is important in analyzing if an asset is a good value as an investment. This applies to corporate finance, bond portfolio management, real estate management, futures trading, forex, and stock investing. There are many different approaches.

The 2007–2009 Stock and Real Estate Market Collapse

The financial crisis started in August of 2007. This was the start of a vicious bear market.

From a theoretical perspective, the crisis lowered "g" in the Gordon Growth model. This drove prices down. This also impacted k_e. Higher uncertainty increased the discount rate, lowering prices again.

Banco Popular (BPOP) was trading over $26 in August of 07'. By August of 2009 the stock traded at $1.63. My wife was fully concentrated in BPOP in her IRA. Ditto for most other BPOP employees.

I instructed my wife to reallocate to the Vanguard S&P 500 index fund (VFINX) at the top of the market. She partially bought back in at the bottom flush with capital.

Indexes dropped by just one third while all other BPOP employees lost their retirement. Her retirement is fast approaching a half a million in value from these two simple decisions she was courageous enough to carry out.

Case: 9/11, Enron and the Market

The 9/11 terrorist attacks and the Enron scandal rocked the stock market in 2001. The Gordon model predicts that the growth rate (g) should drop from post-attack economic paralysis while the required return should rise from risk of both attack and the danger of more miss reported earnings.

This should drive down the price of stocks as measured by an index such as the S&P 500. The price of major indexes fell by 10% that year as the market collapsed for two more years.

PART 2:
Stock Market Indexes

Stock Market Indexes

Stock market indexes measure the price behavior of groups of stocks. Major indexes include the Dow Jones Industrial Average, the S&P 500, and the NASDAQ composite average.

Company	Ticker Symbol	Company	Ticker Symbol
Apple	(NASDAQ:AAPL)	JPMorgan Chase	(NYSE:JPM)
American Express	(NYSE:AXP)	McDonald's	(NYSE:MCD)
Boeing	(NYSE:BA)	3M Company	(NYSE:MMM)
Caterpillar	(NYSE:CAT)	Merck	(NYSE:MRK)
Cisco Systems	(NASDAQ:CSCO)	Microsoft	(NASDAQ:MSFT)
Chevron	(NYSE:CVX)	Nike	(NYSE:NKE)
Coca-Cola	(NYSE:KO)	Pfizer	(NYSE:PFE)
DuPont	(NYSE:DD)	Procter & Gamble	(NYSE:PG)
ExxonMobil	(NYSE:XOM)	The Travelers	(NYSE:TRV)
General Electric	(NYSE:GE)	UnitedHealth	(NYSE:UNH)
Goldman Sachs	(NYSE:GS)	United Technologies	(NYSE:UTX)
Home Depot	(NYSE:HD)	Visa	(NYSE:V)
IBM	(NYSE:IBM)	Verizon	(NYSE:VZ)
Intel	(NASDAQ:INTC)	Wal-Mart	(NYSE:WMT)
Johnson & Johnson	(NYSE:JNJ)	Walt Disney	(NYSE:DIS)

Stock Market Indexes

A dollar invested in the DJIA back in 1980 when the Dow was around 800 would have grown to about $16.40 by 2012 when the DJIA closed that year at 13,104. This represented an annual growth rate of 8.8%. At this rate $100,000 from 1980 is worth $1,640,000 today.

Let's look at the thirty Dow stocks as reported on DogsoftheDow.com in 2017.

Dow Jones Industrial Averages, 1980–1990

Notice that it is critical to (1) buy in low after major crashes, (2) ride out reactions to the major uptrend and (3) get out on indications of a new major crash. In this light buy low and sell high is not so easy.

Dow Jones Industrial Averages, 1990–2013

The DJIA is such a small number of stocks that it can vary widely from a broad index such as the S&P 500. Thus, it is not as widely followed as a barometer as when it was the only index at the beginning of the birth of the modern stock market in New York.

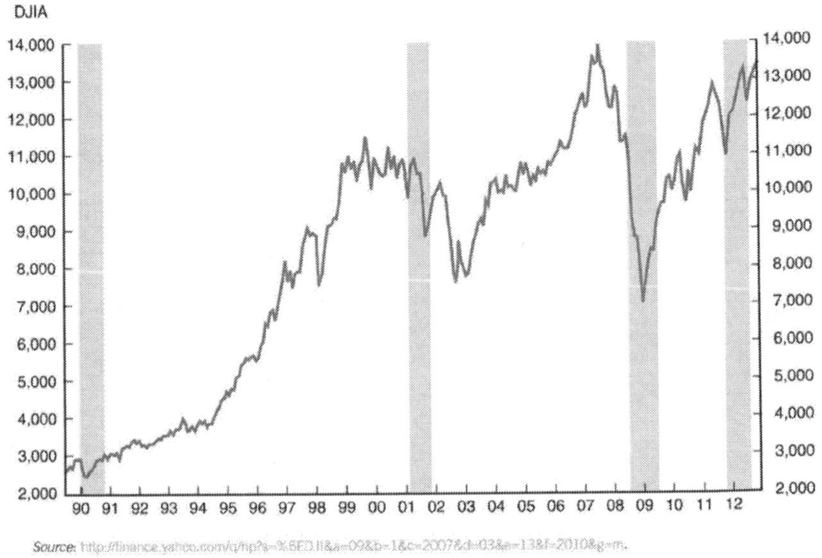

Foreign Stocks

There is an old theory that adding overseas shares to your portfolio will increase returns and reduce volatility. This has not held up.

Do not use ADRs to increase your diversification.

Buying a foreign stock across the home exchange is useful to capture the strong share price surge. However, the purchase may be complicated for American investors due to Italian laws.

The appropriate use of ADRs is to speculate overseas. Look at the chart of Fiat Chrysler Automotive (FCAU).

It operates as an American depository receipt (ADR). This allows the Italian firm to trade on U.S. exchanges, facilitating share purchase. To create FCAU ADR shares U.S. banks buy Italian shares and issue receipts against shares across the NYSE.

The Italian firm must comply with the strict regulatory requirements of the United States to remain listed.

PART 3:
Stock Market Regulation

Stock Market Regulation

The SEC has a primary mission of "*... protect investors and maintain the integrity of the securities markets.*"

The SEC brings as many as 500 actions against individuals and firms in this effort annually through the joint efforts of four divisions.

SEC Divisions

#1: The Division of Corporate Finance is responsible for collecting, reviewing, and archiving all of the documents corporations and individuals must file

#2: The Division of Market Regulation maintains orderly rules and establishes
efficient markets.

#3: The Division of Investment Management focuses on investment management industry oversight and regulation.

#4: The Division of Enforcement investigates rule and regulation violations established by the other divisions.

Instances of dual standards exist in the SEC. And you don't want to be a small fry.

The SEC was heavily criticized for allowing Merrill Lynch to shred millions of documents while investigated.

Summary of Best Diversified Strategies

Indexed IRAs – these are easy to set up. Just buy the lowest cost, lowest turnover equity indexed mutual fund in the menu of selections for your employer sponsored 401(k).

Dogs of the Dow – Discover how to set up a simple 10 stock portfolio at Dogs of the Dow dot com.

The S&P Top Ten Dividend Yielders – Buy the 10 highest dividends yielding stocks in the S&P 500. There are a number of websites such as http://indexarb.com/dividendYieldSortedsp.html that will give you this.

Summary of Best Non-Diversified Focused Strategies

Small Dogs of the Dow – Buy the 5 highest dividend yielding stocks listed at DogsoftheDow.com.

The S&P Five Dividend Yielders – Buy the top 5 dividend yielding stocks at a website such as that in the last slide.

The Warren Buffet 10 Stock Value System – Read all of Warren Buffet's letters to shareholders at

http://www.berkshirehathaway.com/letters/letters.html then buy the 10 best value stocks you can find.

The Charlie Munger 3 Stock Value System – Buy the 3 best value stocks that you can find.

The Nicolas Darvas 3 Stock Price Impact System – I have a course on this.

The Turtle Trading System – I cover this in other courses.

The John Maynard Keynes 1 Stock Portfolio – Buy shares in the biggest and best managed business in the market today that you can find.

The Equity Option Return Amplification Portfolio – Amplify returns 5-fold or more with controlled leverage investing. I have several courses on this.

Summary of Best Investing Books

How I Made $2,000,000 in the Stock Market by Nicolas Darvas – Best description of multiple stock market campaigns. Must read.

Reminiscences of a Stock Operator by Edwin LeFevre – Best description of the mentality of making it big in stocks.

How to Trade Stock by Jesse Livermore – From the legendary stock investor himself interviewed in Reminiscences.

How to Make Money in Stocks: A Winning System in Good Times and Bad by William O'Neil – Good explanations of useful tools from the Investor's Business Daily financial newspaper.

The Dhando Investor by Mohnish Pabrai – Great biography of a bright man from India who made it big after reading all Warren Buffett had to write.

How to Make the Stock Market Make Money for You by Ted Warren – How a welder became vastly wealthy in the stock market.

Summary of Best Psychology Books (cont.)

Think and Grow Rich by Napoleon Hill — How to build focus and resolve.

The Disappearance of the Universe by Gary Renard — How to look at money differently for a winning mentality by letting go of material concerns. Very helpful when the market goes against you.

Advaita Vedanta : A Philosophical Reconstruction — A similar system of thought as that described by Gary Renard.

Student Activity Challenge

Find the stock you consider the single best among the Dogs of the Dow today. Use DogsOfTheDow.com to do your research. Post in the discussion board of the free online version of this training and I will critique. The student with the highest rising stock at the end of the month wins a prize. Enroll in the free online training at http://worryfreewealth.com/offers/

-Doc Brown

Made in the USA
Monee, IL
04 November 2026

67375600R00022